Samsung Galaxy S25 Ultra User Guide

Beginner and Senior-Friendly Guide to Mastering Your Device with Practical Tips to Unlock Its Full Potential

Melissa M. Juarez

Disclaimer

The information provided in this book is intended for general informational purposes only. While every effort has been made to ensure the accuracy and reliability of the content, the author and publisher make no representations or warranties regarding the completeness, accuracy, or suitability of the information for any particular purpose.

All brand names, product names, and trademarks used in this book are the property of their respective owners. The author is not affiliated with any of the brands, companies, or third-party services mentioned, and the inclusion of any brand, product, or service does not imply endorsement or recommendation.

The advice and recommendations in this book are based on the knowledge and research available at the time of publication. However, the technology industry is constantly evolving, and updates, changes, or new developments may occur that are not reflected in this text. The author and publisher are not responsible for any loss, damage, or inconvenience caused by the use of any information or recommendations contained within this book. Readers are encouraged to verify any information and consult with a qualified professional or expert before making decisions based on the content.

By reading this book, you acknowledge that the author and publisher are not liable for any damages or consequences arising from the use of this information.

Contents

Introduction

Galaxy S25 Ultra—Your Gateway to Innovation

The Galaxy S25 Ultra is not just another smartphone—it's a leap into the future of technology, designed to enhance every aspect of your digital life. With cutting-edge features and groundbreaking innovations, this device redefines what a smartphone can do. Here's why the Galaxy S25 Ultra is your ultimate tool for staying ahead of the curve.

Advanced AI Integration

At the heart of the Galaxy S25 Ultra is Samsung's latest AI advancements, ensuring your phone is smarter and more responsive than ever before. The Now Brief feature, for instance, learns your daily patterns and provides real-time, context-aware notifications and suggestions, streamlining your productivity. Whether you're in a meeting, at a café, or traveling, the phone adapts to your needs, keeping you organized without lifting a finger.

Enhanced Performance

With the new Snapdragon 8 Elite processor, the Galaxy S25 Ultra pushes the boundaries of speed and efficiency. It's 37% faster on the CPU and 40% quicker on the NPU, meaning apps open instantly, multitasking is seamless, and your gaming experience is more fluid than ever. No more lag, no more waiting—just pure performance. Whether you're tackling complex tasks or enjoying high-quality games, the S25 Ultra will keep up with your pace.

Superior Display Technology

The 6.9-inch Quad HD+ AMOLED display is nothing short of stunning. With minimal bezels, the screen is expansive, offering vibrant visuals that make everything come to life. Whether you're watching movies, editing photos, or sketching your next big idea, the S25 Ultra's display immerses you in crystal-clear detail. Expect richer colors, deeper contrasts, and an all-around more engaging viewing experience.

Robust Durability

Smartphones need to be built to last, and the Galaxy S25 Ultra is engineered to withstand the test of time. The titanium frame and Corning Gorilla Glass Armor 2 ensure this device can handle the rigors of everyday use, from accidental drops to harsh environments. The S25 Ultra is built for longevity, combining resilience with style.

Comprehensive Software Support

The S25 Ultra runs on Android 15 with Samsung's One UI 7, delivering an intuitive and easy-to-use interface. But what sets it apart is Samsung's commitment to long-term support, offering up to seven years of software updates. This means you'll have access to the latest features, security patches, and performance enhancements long after you've made the purchase.

The Galaxy S25 Ultra isn't just a smartphone—it's a powerhouse that will elevate your tech experience to new heights. Ready to embrace the future? With the Galaxy S25 Ultra, the future is now.

How This Guide Will Help You Master Your Device

This guide is designed to help you unlock the full potential of your Galaxy S25 Ultra, regardless of your technical expertise. Whether you're a first-time smartphone user or a seasoned pro, you'll find everything you need to make the most out of your device. Here's how this guide will support your journey:

Step-by-Step Instructions

Each chapter is carefully crafted with clear, step-by-step instructions that guide you through every feature and setting on the Galaxy S25 Ultra. Whether you're learning the basics or exploring advanced functions, these instructions ensure that you can confidently navigate and personalize your device. You won't have to guess or search for answers—everything is laid out simply, so you can follow along at your own pace.

Practical Tips and Tricks

As you explore the Galaxy S25 Ultra's vast range of features, we'll share expert tips and shortcuts that will enhance your experience. Whether it's streamlining your app usage, taking better photos, or boosting battery life, these insider insights will help you get the most out of your phone without wasting time.

Troubleshooting Guidance

No device is perfect, but don't worry—we've got you covered. This guide offers practical troubleshooting solutions for common issues you might encounter, from connectivity problems to app glitches. You'll feel empowered to resolve any challenges on your own, without needing to call for support or visit a service center.

Regular Updates

The world of technology moves fast, and so does your Galaxy S25 Ultra. To ensure this guide remains relevant, we'll provide regular updates that reflect the latest software releases and feature enhancements. This means you'll always have access to the most current information, keeping your device running smoothly and up-to-date.

With this guide, you'll gain the confidence and knowledge to master every aspect of your Galaxy S25 Ultra. We'll walk you through the basics and dive deep into advanced features, ensuring that you always have the tools to make the most of your device.

Who This Guide Is For: Beginners and Experienced Users Alike

This guide is designed to be your ultimate companion, regardless of where you are in your smartphone journey. Whether you're just getting started or you've been using smartphones for years, the Galaxy S25 Ultra's powerful features and innovations will open up new possibilities. Here's how this guide serves a wide range of readers:

Beginners

If you're new to smartphones, don't worry—we've got you covered. This guide takes you through the basics, ensuring you understand how to get started with your Galaxy S25 Ultra.

From setting up your device to learning essential features, we provide clear, simple instructions that will help you build confidence as you navigate your new device. You'll be up and running in no time.

Experienced Users

For those who have been using smartphones for a while, this guide goes deeper. It provides in-depth insights into the Galaxy S25 Ultra's advanced capabilities, from optimizing performance to exploring hidden features. If you're looking to push your device to its limits, you'll find tips and techniques to unlock its full potential.

Tech Enthusiasts

Are you someone who loves to stay ahead of the curve when it comes to technology? This guide will appeal to you. It explores the latest innovations, including AI integrations, display technologies, and powerful performance features that set the Galaxy S25 Ultra apart. Dive deep into the tech that makes this device a game-changer and discover how it's shaping the future of smartphones.

Professionals

The Galaxy S25 Ultra is not just a phone—it's a productivity powerhouse. This guide highlights features that professionals will find invaluable, such as productivity tools, multitasking options, and customization features that help you get work done efficiently. Whether you're managing emails, working on presentations, or organizing your calendar, this device has everything you need to stay productive on the go.

Seniors

For older adults, we've included sections focused on accessibility and simplified instructions. We know that smartphones can sometimes feel overwhelming, but with this guide, we ensure a smooth, user-friendly experience. From larger text options to easy navigation tips, the Galaxy S25 Ultra will become an intuitive tool that enhances everyday life.

Chapter 1

Getting Started with the Galaxy S25 Ultra

Getting started with your new Galaxy S25 Ultra should be a smooth and exciting experience. In this section, we'll walk you through the unboxing and initial setup process, making sure your device is ready to go and tailored to your preferences from the start.

Unboxing the Device

When you open the Galaxy S25 Ultra box, you'll find everything you need to get started:

- The Galaxy S25 Ultra device
- S Pen (color-matched to your device)
- USB-C cable for charging and data transfer
- User manual for quick reference

The **S Pen** is a standout feature of this model. It's neatly tucked into the lower side of the device, and it fits perfectly into the frame, so you won't need to worry about misplacing it. The attention to detail in the packaging ensures that your new device is well-protected and ready to use.

Inserting the SIM Card

To insert your SIM card:

1. Use the ejector tool provided in the box to open the SIM tray.
2. Place your SIM card into the tray, making sure it's aligned correctly.
3. Carefully reinsert the tray back into the device.

Ensure the tray is securely closed, as this helps maintain the water resistance of your Galaxy S25 Ultra.

Powering On the Device

Now it's time to power on your device. Here's how:

1. Press and hold the side button until the Samsung logo appears on the screen.
2. Follow the on-screen instructions to:
   - Select your language
   - Connect to Wi-Fi
   - Sign in to your Google and Samsung accounts for a seamless experience.

Restoring Data

If you're upgrading from a previous device, this is the perfect time to restore your apps, settings, and data. During setup, you'll be prompted to restore your data using either your Google account or Samsung account. This process helps transfer everything you need to start using your new device without losing any important information.

Completing Setup

Once the basic setup is complete, you're ready to dive deeper into personalizing your Galaxy S25 Ultra. Explore the settings and features to tailor the device to your needs. Whether it's adjusting display preferences, enabling accessibility options, or customizing the home screen layout, your phone is now fully set up and ready to adapt to your lifestyle.

Key Features of the Galaxy S25 Ultra Explained

The Galaxy S25 Ultra is packed with advanced features designed to enhance your smartphone experience. From its stunning display to its powerful AI integration, this device is built to deliver seamless performance, making it a true standout in the market. Let's dive into the key features that make the Galaxy S25 Ultra so exceptional:

Display

The 6.9-inch Dynamic AMOLED 2X display is a visual treat, offering vibrant colors and deep contrasts that bring your content to life. The 120Hz adaptive refresh rate ensures smooth scrolling and a fluid response, whether you're browsing, gaming, or watching videos. It's a screen designed for those who appreciate stunning visuals and a truly immersive viewing experience.

Processor

At the heart of the Galaxy S25 Ultra is the Snapdragon 8 Elite for Galaxy chipset. This powerhouse ensures smooth multitasking, lightning-fast app launches, and a responsive experience. Whether you're juggling multiple apps or playing high-performance games, the S25 Ultra handles it with ease, ensuring you never miss a beat.

Camera System

With the quad-camera setup, including a 200MP wide lens, a 50MP ultra-wide lens, and dual telephoto lenses, the Galaxy S25 Ultra brings professional-grade photography right to your pocket. Capture stunning details, vibrant landscapes, and breathtaking portraits with ease. The advanced camera features make it easier than ever to shoot like a pro, no matter your skill level.

Battery Life

The 5000mAh battery is designed to keep you going throughout the day. Paired with 45W fast charging and Qi2 wireless charging, you won't have to worry about running out of power. Whether you need a quick charge or prefer wireless convenience, the S25 Ultra has you covered with long-lasting power.

Design and Build

Crafted with a titanium frame and Corning Gorilla Armor 2 glass, the S25 Ultra is built for durability. It's sleek, stylish, and tough enough to handle daily wear and tear, ensuring that your phone stays looking great and performing well over time.

AI Integration

Smart features like Now Brief and Cross-App Action use advanced AI to make your phone experience smoother and more efficient. Whether it's providing real-time, context-aware notifications or automating tasks, the Galaxy S25 Ultra adapts to your needs, offering smart assistance whenever you need it.

S Pen

The built-in S Pen adds precision to your interactions, allowing for accurate note-taking, sketching, and navigation. Whether you're jotting down ideas or editing photos, the S Pen provides a level of control that elevates your experience.

Software

Running on Android 15 with One UI 7, the Galaxy S25 Ultra offers a user-friendly interface that's intuitive and easy to navigate. With plenty of customization options, you can tailor your device to match your preferences, ensuring it's as personal as it is powerful.

Personalizing Your Device: Customizing the Home Screen

Personalizing your home screen is one of the most exciting ways to make your device feel like it's truly yours. With just a few simple tweaks, you can transform your home screen into a workspace that suits your style and improves your efficiency. Here's how to do it.

Organizing Apps

Start by grouping your apps into folders to create a more organized layout. For example, you can place all your social media apps in one folder, like "Social," while keeping work-related apps under "Productivity." This will help reduce clutter and make it easier to find what you need.

Using Widgets

Widgets provide you with at-a-glance information, helping you stay updated without opening an app. Add widgets for your most-used functions, such as weather updates, upcoming calendar events, or breaking news. Simply tap and hold an empty area on your home screen, select "Widgets," and choose the ones that best fit your needs.

Adjusting Icon Sizes and Layout

Sometimes the default icon size doesn't suit your preferences. You can resize icons and adjust the grid layout to either fit more apps on your screen or to create a cleaner, more minimalist look. To do this, go to your home screen settings and select your preferred size and grid options.

Setting Wallpapers and Themes

The wallpaper and theme you choose will set the overall vibe of your device. Whether you prefer a calming background or a vibrant design, you can easily change the wallpaper by tapping and holding the screen, then selecting "Wallpapers" or "Themes." Pick one that reflects your personal taste.

Enabling Edge Panels

Edge Panels are a convenient way to access your most-used apps, contacts, or tools without cluttering your main home screen. You can enable Edge Panels by going to your settings and turning them on. Once activated, swipe from the edge of your screen to reveal quick shortcuts.

Customizing the Lock Screen

Your lock screen doesn't have to be plain. You can adjust the clock style, add shortcuts, and even include widgets, so you can quickly access information without unlocking your device. Head to your lock screen settings, and personalize it to suit your preferences.

By making these simple adjustments, you'll not only make your device more visually appealing but also improve its functionality to fit your unique needs.

Navigating the Galaxy S25 Ultra Interface: Icons, Shortcuts, and Gestures

The Galaxy S25 Ultra offers a user-friendly interface, designed to make navigation intuitive and efficient. By mastering a few simple gestures and shortcuts, you'll be able to navigate your device seamlessly and get the most out of its powerful features.

Understanding the Home Screen Layout

Your home screen is where the magic happens. It consists of several key elements: the status bar at the top, where you can see notifications and battery status; your home screen, where apps and widgets are located; and the app icons that give you quick access to your most-used apps. You can rearrange apps by holding an icon and dragging it to your preferred spot or into folders to create a cleaner, more organized layout.

Using Touch Gestures

Gestures are key to a smooth navigation experience. Here's how to use them:

- **Swipe-up**: Open the multitasking view to see all your open apps.
- **Swipe-down**: Access your notifications and quick settings.
- **Swipe-right**: Open the Edge Panel for quick shortcuts to apps, contacts, or tools. These gestures help you navigate without ever needing to press physical buttons, making it faster and more fluid.

Navigation Bar and Button Customization

You can choose between on-screen buttons or gesture-based navigation. Gesture navigation provides a more immersive experience, but if you prefer the traditional on-screen buttons, you can customize the navigation bar to suit your preferences. To make the switch, go to Settings > Display > Navigation Bar and choose the option you prefer.

App Shortcuts and Quick Actions

App shortcuts are a fantastic time-saver. Simply long-press an app icon to reveal options like creating a new message, opening the camera, or accessing settings. These shortcuts make it easy to jump straight into the app's key features.

Using the App Drawer

To access the app drawer, simply swipe up from the bottom of the home screen. From here, you can organize apps into folders or categories, and even hide certain apps for a cleaner interface. This keeps your home screen focused on what matters most.

Edge Panel Navigation

The Edge Panel gives you quick access to your favorite apps, contacts, and tools. You can easily swipe from the edge of the screen to open it, then swipe again to customize it. This feature is perfect for multitaskers and those who prefer fast access to important functions.

Multitasking and Split-Screen Mode

The Galaxy S25 Ultra lets you use split-screen mode to multitask. For example, you can browse the web while chatting in a messaging app. Simply open the multitasking view, select an app, and drag it to the top or bottom of the screen. The pop-up view is another useful feature for keeping multiple apps in small windows for easy access.

Setting Up and Using Voice Commands

Samsung's voice assistant, Bixby, allows you to perform tasks hands-free. Activate Bixby by saying, "Hi, Bixby" or by pressing and holding the Bixby button. You can use voice commands to send messages, set reminders, open apps, and more. If Bixby doesn't always understand you, train it to improve its voice recognition by going to Settings > Bixby > Voice Wake-up.

Mastering these basic features will make your Galaxy S25 Ultra easier to navigate and more efficient to use. Try these steps out and see how much quicker and smoother your experience becomes.

Chapter 2

Exploring the Software and User Interface

Android 14 and Samsung One UI: The Power Behind Your Device

Android 15 and Samsung One UI 7 bring powerful features and enhancements that not only optimize your device's performance but also make it more user-friendly, secure, and personalized. Here's an overview of the key features and how they can improve your experience with your Galaxy S25 Ultra.

Android 15 Features

Android 15 focuses on enhanced security and privacy without compromising user experience. One standout feature is on-device live scanning, which runs locally on your device to check app activity for phishing and other deceptive behaviors. This feature ensures your device remains protected while safeguarding your privacy. Now, you can feel more secure knowing that your data isn't being sent to external servers for scanning.

One UI 7 Enhancements

Samsung's One UI 7 introduces a range of design tweaks and usability improvements, making it easier to personalize your device to fit your needs. The home screen has been simplified for a cleaner look, while redesigned widgets make it simpler to view and manage key information at a glance. Additionally, the customizable lock screen allows you to adjust the clock style and add widgets for quick access to your favorite features. One UI 7 helps streamline your device's interface, providing a more intuitive experience.

AI Integration

With the integration of Galaxy AI, tasks across apps have become easier than ever. Features like the Now Bar and Seamless Actions enable you to perform tasks with just a single command. Whether you're switching between apps or performing a multi-step action, these AI features allow you to accomplish things more efficiently, saving you time throughout your day.

Security and Privacy

Android 15 takes your security and privacy seriously with several new features. For example, private space isolates sensitive data, ensuring that it remains secure from unauthorized access. Another great addition is the ability to control remote speaker volume using your phone's volume buttons—no need to unlock or open your device. This simple feature enhances convenience while maintaining privacy.

These advancements in Android 15 and One UI 7 bring the power of security, ease of use, and personalization to your device, helping you get the most out of your Galaxy S25 Ultra.

Navigating Your Device: The Essentials of Touch Gestures, Menus, and Settings

Navigating your Galaxy S25 Ultra becomes second nature once you're familiar with the core touch gestures, menus, and settings. These features are designed to make your device more intuitive and efficient. Here's how to master them.

Touch Gestures

Gestures are key to fluid navigation on your device. Here are a few essential gestures that will make using your Galaxy S25 Ultra much quicker and easier:

- **Swipe up**: Open the app drawer, where all your installed apps are listed.
- **Swipe down**: Access the notifications panel to view updates and toggle quick settings like Wi-Fi and Bluetooth.
- **Pinch to zoom**: Zoom in or out on images, maps, or webpages by placing two fingers on the screen and moving them apart or together.

These gestures allow you to navigate your device efficiently without relying on physical buttons.

Menus and Settings

The Settings app is organized into categories like Connections, Display, and Privacy, making it easy to find and adjust your preferences. For example, if you want to change your display settings, simply tap on Display in the menu.

If you're having trouble connecting to Wi-Fi, go to Connections to troubleshoot. Understanding this structure helps you quickly locate the setting you're looking for, saving you time and frustration.

Quick Settings Panel

The Quick Settings panel gives you fast access to key functions like Wi-Fi, Bluetooth, and Do Not Disturb mode. To open it, swipe down from the top of your screen. From here, you can toggle these features on or off with just one tap, giving you quick control over the most-used settings.

Search Functionality

Not sure where to find a specific setting? Use the search bar in the Settings app to quickly locate it. Instead of scrolling through the menu, just type in the setting you're looking for, and it will pop up in the search results. This is especially useful for advanced features or less frequently used options.

Accessibility Features

Samsung's Galaxy S25 Ultra includes several accessibility options to make the device more user-friendly. These include magnification gestures, screen readers, and high-contrast themes. You can enable these features in the Accessibility menu within the Settings app to tailor the device to your needs.

By mastering these essential gestures, menus, and settings, you'll be able to navigate your Galaxy S25 Ultra like a pro, making the most of its powerful features.

Managing Apps and Software Updates for a Smooth Experience

Keeping your Galaxy S25 Ultra in top shape requires proactive management of apps and software updates. By following these straightforward steps, you can optimize your device's performance, maintain security, and ensure it runs smoothly.

App Management

Over time, unused apps can clutter your device and take up valuable storage space. To keep your device running efficiently, make it a habit to regularly review your installed apps. Uninstall any apps you no longer use by going to Settings > Apps, selecting the app, and tapping Uninstall. This frees up storage and can help improve overall device performance.

App Permissions

Your apps may request access to sensitive data like your contacts, location, or camera. Managing app permissions can enhance your privacy and security. To adjust these settings, go to Settings > Apps > [App Name] > Permissions. Here, you can decide which permissions each app should have, limiting access to only the necessary features.

Software Updates

Enabling automatic updates is an easy way to keep your Galaxy S25 Ultra up-to-date. This ensures that the device receives the latest features, bug fixes, and security patches without requiring manual intervention. To enable this, go to Settings > Software Update, and toggle Auto Download Over Wi-Fi to keep your device updated automatically.

Update Notifications

Even with automatic updates enabled, it's important to keep an eye on update notifications. These alerts provide valuable information about new features, improvements, and security fixes. Before installing any updates, review the details to understand what's changing and ensure you're prepared for any new features or changes.

Beta Programs

If you're curious about new features and don't mind taking a little risk, consider participating in beta programs. These programs let you test new features before they're officially released. However, beta versions may have bugs, so it's important to understand that you might encounter some instability. To join, look for beta program invitations through Samsung Members or the Google Play Store.

By following these simple tips for managing apps and updates, you'll help ensure your Galaxy S25 Ultra remains secure, efficient, and up-to-date.

Samsung Knox: How to Keep Your Data Safe with Samsung's Security Suite

Samsung Knox is a robust security suite designed to protect your device and personal data from potential threats. Whether you're looking to secure sensitive information or prevent unauthorized access, Knox provides an array of features to ensure your data stays safe.

Knox Security Features

Samsung Knox offers real-time protection by monitoring your device's behavior and controlling access to prevent data breaches. It keeps track of your device's integrity, ensuring that it remains secure against unauthorized changes and malicious attacks. This feature is especially valuable for those who need additional peace of mind regarding their device's security.

Secure Folder

For sensitive information, Secure Folder offers a private, encrypted space where you can store apps, photos, documents, and other personal data. Think of it as a vault on your phone—anything placed in the Secure Folder is protected with its own PIN, password, or biometric authentication, ensuring that only you can access it.

Remote Management

If you're managing a fleet of devices or need to secure a company-issued phone, Knox provides remote management capabilities for IT administrators. This feature allows remote enforcement of security policies, app installations, and device configurations, making it easier for businesses to maintain secure devices without physical access.

Biometric Authentication

Samsung Knox integrates with advanced biometric security features like fingerprint scanning and facial recognition, providing a secure, user-friendly way to unlock your device. These features ensure that only authorized users can access your device, making it far more difficult for unauthorized individuals to gain entry.

Knox Guard

If your device is lost or stolen, Knox Guard can lock it down, rendering it unusable by unauthorized users. You can also remotely wipe the device to protect your sensitive information, ensuring that nothing valuable is left behind.

Knox Mobile Enrollment

For businesses that manage multiple devices, Knox Mobile Enrollment simplifies the setup process. It automatically configures devices with the necessary security protocols when they are enrolled in a company's system, streamlining device management and ensuring that all devices are secure right out of the box.

Samsung Knox for Enterprise

For business users, Knox for Enterprise provides additional security layers for managing devices securely. It includes features like app control, device encryption, and secure communications, ensuring that enterprise data is fully protected across all devices.

Knox Vault

For the utmost protection of your most sensitive information, Knox Vault isolates data like passwords and authentication keys in a dedicated, hardware-encrypted space. This makes it resistant to software-based attacks, providing an extra level of security for users who frequently handle online transactions or store important information on their devices.

By enabling these Knox features, you can significantly enhance your device's security and keep your personal and business data protected from a wide range of threats.

Chapter 3

Getting the Most Out of Your Camera

Understanding the Galaxy S25 Ultra's Quad-Camera System

The Galaxy S25 Ultra's quad-camera system provides a versatile range of lenses, each designed to capture stunning photos in different scenarios. Whether you're shooting wide landscapes, detailed portraits, or close-ups, the S25 Ultra has you covered with its powerful camera setup.

Main Camera

At the heart of the camera system is the 200MP wide-angle lens. With an f/1.7 aperture, 24mm focal length, and a 1/1.3" sensor size, this camera delivers exceptional detail, making it ideal for capturing everything from stunning landscapes to intricate close-ups. The high resolution ensures that even after cropping, your photos retain sharpness and clarity.

Ultra-Wide Lens

The 50MP ultra-wide lens on the Galaxy S25 Ultra has a 120° field of view and an f/1.9 aperture, allowing you to capture expansive scenes with minimal distortion. Whether you're photographing large architectural structures or sweeping landscapes, this lens ensures your shots maintain a sense of depth and perspective.

Telephoto Lenses
The S25 Ultra features two telephoto lenses, each designed to give you more flexibility for zoomed-in shots.

- **3x Optical Zoom Lens**: This 10MP lens has an f/2.4 aperture and 67mm focal length, perfect for portrait shots and medium-distance photography, delivering clear, crisp images with natural background blur.
- **5x Periscope Telephoto Lens**: For even more zoom, the 50MP periscope telephoto lens has an f/3.4 aperture and 111mm focal length, offering 5x optical zoom with minimal loss of image quality, ensuring detailed shots even at longer distances.

Front Camera

For selfies and video calls, the Galaxy S25 Ultra's 12MP front camera is equipped with an f/2.2 aperture and 26mm focal length, capturing bright, clear, and detailed self-portraits or group shots with ease.

Each of these lenses works together to ensure that you're always prepared to capture the best possible shot, whether you're zooming in on a distant subject or photographing a wide-open scene. The S25 Ultra's camera system is truly designed to give you professional-grade quality in the palm of your hand.

Pro Tips for Capturing Stunning Photos and Videos

Maximizing the potential of your Galaxy S25 Ultra's camera system is easy with a few expert techniques. These tips will help you elevate your photography and videography, allowing you to capture stunning images and smooth videos with ease.

Utilize Pro Mode

Unlock full creative control by using Pro Mode. This mode lets you manually adjust settings such as ISO, shutter speed, focus, and white balance. Whether you're capturing fast-moving subjects or shooting in challenging lighting, Pro Mode gives you the flexibility to fine-tune each aspect of your shot for professional-quality results.

Master Focus Techniques

For sharp, crisp photos, especially in macro or portrait photography, use the touch focus or manual focus settings. Tap on your subject on the screen to ensure it's in focus, or adjust the focus manually for more precise control. This is essential for creating striking, detailed shots where the subject stands out.

Optimize Exposure Settings

Exposure compensation allows you to adjust the brightness of your photos, ensuring well-lit images even in tricky lighting conditions. If your photo is too dark or too bright, swipe up or down on the exposure bar to find the right balance, especially when shooting against strong backlighting or in dim environments.

Explore Night Mode

Night Mode is a game-changer for low-light photography. It combines multiple exposures to increase brightness and enhance detail. For clear, sharp images in dark environments, activate Night Mode to capture more light and reveal the true colors of your subject.

Leverage AI Features

Enable AI enhancements like Scene Optimizer and Shot Suggestions to automatically adjust settings for the best results based on the scene or subject. These features intelligently optimize your settings, ensuring optimal color, contrast, and sharpness with minimal effort on your part.

Stabilize Your Shots

For smooth, shake-free videos, use the Super Steady mode. For even better stability, consider using a tripod or gimbal to minimize motion blur and achieve professional-looking footage, especially for action shots or when filming on the go.

Experiment with Composition

Good composition can make all the difference. Use techniques like the rule of thirds, leading lines, and framing to guide the viewer's eye and create more visually compelling photos. These simple tips help you create balanced and engaging images.

Regularly Clean Your Lenses

Ensure your shots are clear by regularly cleaning your camera lenses. Dirt and fingerprints can blur your photos, so take a moment to wipe the lenses with a microfiber cloth before each shoot for crisp, sharp images.

By following these tips, you can take your photography and videography to the next level, capturing breathtaking moments with your Galaxy S25 Ultra.

Editing Tools and Modes: Master Pro Mode and More

With the Galaxy S25 Ultra, your creativity doesn't end after capturing a photo or video. The powerful editing tools and modes available on your device allow you to refine and personalize your content, giving it a professional touch with ease. Here's how you can elevate your images and videos.

Pro Mode Editing

After capturing images in Pro Mode, you can fine-tune various settings such as exposure, contrast, and saturation using the in-built editor. This gives you full control to adjust the look of your photos, ensuring you get exactly what you envision. Whether you want to enhance the colors or adjust the brightness, these tools help you perfect your shots.

Expert RAW Mode

For users looking for more flexibility in post-processing, Expert RAW Mode captures images in RAW format, allowing you to work with unprocessed image data. This offers greater flexibility for professional-grade edits, giving you control over the details that other formats might compress or lose.

Video Editing Suite

The video editor lets you create polished videos directly from your Galaxy S25 Ultra. You can easily trim clips, adjust playback speed, apply filters, and add music to enhance your videos. This built-in tool is ideal for making quick edits and producing videos that are ready to share.

AR Doodle and Stickers

Add a fun, interactive touch to your photos and videos with AR Doodles and stickers. You can draw doodles, add stickers, or even insert text, making your content more personalized and engaging. This is a great way to create memorable, creative content that stands out.

Bixby Vision Integration

With Bixby Vision, you can enhance your editing process by translating text, scanning QR codes, or identifying objects and landmarks directly through the camera app. You can overlay text or extra details on your photos or videos, making them more informative or context-rich.

Portrait Mode Editing

After capturing a portrait, you can refine the blur effect and adjust the lighting and background using advanced editing tools. Modes like Studio Lighting and Natural Light allow you to create professional-looking portraits by adjusting the lighting to highlight your subject and add depth to the photo.

Filters and Presets

To give your photos a specific mood, use built-in filters or download additional ones from the Galaxy Store. Filters can enhance color tones, add vintage effects, or provide high-contrast looks, allowing you to express your artistic vision.

AI Editing Features

Samsung's AI-based editing tools automatically enhance your photos by adjusting color balance, sharpness, and brightness based on the scene. Additionally, AI can help remove unwanted objects from your photos, making the editing process quick and hassle-free.

With these tools at your fingertips, editing photos and videos becomes a fun and creative experience. Whether you're a beginner or a seasoned pro, the Galaxy S25 Ultra makes it easy to transform your content into something amazing.

Using the Camera for Content Creation and Professional Photography

The Galaxy S25 Ultra's camera system is not only designed for everyday use—it's a powerful tool for content creation and professional photography. Whether you're capturing high-quality social media posts or shooting a detailed product photo, the S25 Ultra offers the flexibility and features to take your work to the next level. Here's how to make the most of its capabilities.

Content Creation for Social Media

With the 200MP camera and advanced AI features, the Galaxy S25 Ultra lets you create vibrant, high-quality images perfect for social media platforms like Instagram, TikTok, and YouTube. The camera ensures your photos stand out in any feed with exceptional detail and clarity. When capturing vertical content, consider using the portrait mode for sharp, professional-looking shots. For 4K video, take advantage of the camera's video recording capabilities to ensure your clips are crisp and clear.

Vlogging and Video Content

The 4K 60fps recording capability is perfect for creating high-quality vlogs. Even when you're on the move, the camera's advanced stabilization and noise reduction ensure smooth, professional videos. Use the 5x telephoto lens to add variety with dynamic zoom shots, capturing close-ups or distant scenes with ease. Whether you're filming action or providing commentary, these features will enhance the quality of your video content.

Professional Photography Techniques

For professional-grade photos, the Pro RAW mode gives you complete control over your images. Shooting in RAW format captures unprocessed data, allowing for detailed editing and adjustment in post-production. The camera's wide, ultra-wide, and telephoto lenses let you cover a wide range of photography scenarios, from sweeping landscapes to fine details, making it versatile for various types of professional work.

Product Photography

The ultra-wide lens is excellent for capturing clear product shots, while the camera's macro capabilities let you take stunning close-ups with crisp detail. To make your products stand out, experiment with different lighting setups and composition techniques. Adjust your camera's settings to ensure that the items are highlighted in the best possible light, creating attractive visuals that draw attention.

Event and Portrait Photography

Capture events such as weddings or professional headshots with the portrait mode. This feature allows you to create stunning bokeh effects and maintain sharp focus on the subject, making portraits look natural and professional. The 50MP wide-angle lens is ideal for group shots in busy environments, ensuring that everyone is clearly visible and in focus.

Editing for Content Creation

The built-in editing tools allow you to enhance your photos and videos right from your Galaxy S25 Ultra. You can adjust exposure, enhance colors, apply filters, and even edit video footage to create polished content. Advanced editing features like object removal or montage creation allow for a professional touch, perfect for content that will be shared with clients or posted on social media.

With these techniques and the power of the Galaxy S25 Ultra's camera, you're equipped to create stunning content and professional-quality photos and videos. Whether for social media or client work, this device has everything you need to produce eye-catching visuals.

Chapter 4

Maximizing Battery Life and Performance

Managing Battery Health: Tips for Long-Lasting Battery Use

To ensure your Galaxy S25 Ultra's battery remains efficient over time, adopting a few simple habits and settings can make a significant difference. Here are some tips to help you maximize battery life and keep your device running smoothly.

Avoid Full Discharges

Regularly draining your battery to 0% can shorten its lifespan. Instead, aim to keep your battery level between 20% and 80% for optimal health. This prevents over-stressing the battery, allowing it to maintain a longer lifespan and perform better over time.

Use Adaptive Charging

Enable the "Protect Battery" feature to limit charging to 85%. This reduces the strain on your battery during overnight charging, preventing it from staying at full capacity for extended periods, which can contribute to wear. Adaptive charging helps keep your battery healthy in the long run.

Maintain Optimal Temperature

Keep your device within the recommended temperature range of 0°C to 35°C (32°F to 95°F). Exposure to extreme heat or cold can negatively impact battery performance and longevity. Avoid leaving your device in hot cars or exposing it to direct sunlight for prolonged periods.

Regularly Update Software

Keep your device updated with the latest software updates. Manufacturers often release updates that include optimizations for battery performance, improving efficiency and reducing unnecessary power consumption. Check for updates regularly in your device's Settings to ensure it's running the latest version.

Monitor Battery Usage

Use the built-in battery usage tools to track which apps consume the most power. If you notice certain apps using excessive battery, you can adjust their settings or limit their usage. By staying mindful of battery usage, you can prevent unnecessary drain and extend battery life.

By incorporating these simple habits and settings into your routine, you'll help prolong your Galaxy S25 Ultra's battery health and ensure your device continues to perform at its best.

Optimizing Battery with Power Saving Modes and Charging Tips

Maximizing your Galaxy S25 Ultra's battery life throughout the day requires a combination of smart charging practices and utilizing the device's built-in power-saving features. Follow these steps to make sure your device lasts longer without compromising its performance.

Activate Power Saving Modes

To extend battery life, activate the Power Saving Mode by navigating to Settings > Battery > Power Saving Mode. This mode reduces background activity, dims the screen, and limits app usage to help conserve power throughout the day. It's a quick and effective way to get more use from your battery when you need it most.

Adjust Performance Profiles

In Device Care, you can select a "Lite" performance profile to reduce the workload on your CPU and GPU. This lowers energy consumption while still allowing the device to run smoothly for everyday tasks. This is particularly helpful when you want to conserve battery without sacrificing basic functionality.

Disable Unnecessary Features

Features like Bluetooth, GPS, and Wi-Fi can drain your battery if left on unnecessarily. Make sure to turn them off when you're not using them. You can do this quickly from the Quick Settings panel or go to Settings to disable them manually. This small adjustment helps prevent excess power consumption.

Optimize Screen Settings

The screen is one of the largest power consumers on your device. To reduce its energy consumption, lower the screen brightness and set a shorter screen timeout. This ensures the screen doesn't stay on longer than needed, and by dimming it, you'll save battery throughout the day.

Use Dark Mode

Activating Dark Mode can help reduce battery usage, especially on OLED screens like the one on your Galaxy S25 Ultra. Darker pixels require less power to display, so switching to Dark Mode can save energy and extend battery life, particularly when using apps with a lot of white or bright backgrounds.

By applying these power-saving strategies, you can ensure that your Galaxy S25 Ultra lasts longer, whether you're working, traveling, or enjoying entertainment.

Troubleshooting Battery Issues and Boosting Performance

If you're experiencing battery issues with your Galaxy S25 Ultra, don't worry—there are several simple steps you can take to identify and resolve the problem. Here's a practical troubleshooting guide to help you get your device back to optimal performance.

Check Battery Usage Statistics

Start by checking which apps are consuming the most power. To do this, go to Settings > Battery and review the Battery Usage section. This will show you how much battery each app is using. If an app is draining battery excessively, consider limiting its usage or adjusting its settings to reduce its power consumption.

Clear Cache Partition

Sometimes, temporary files can accumulate and affect your device's performance. To clear these files, reboot your device into recovery mode and select the option to wipe the cache partition. This won't delete your data, but it will remove unnecessary files that might be slowing your device down.

Perform a Factory Reset

If battery problems persist, consider performing a factory reset. First, back up your data to ensure you don't lose important files, as this will erase all data from your device. After the reset, your phone will be restored to its original settings, which can resolve any software-related issues affecting battery performance.

Update Apps and Software

Ensure that both your apps and the device's operating system are up to date. Updates often include bug fixes and optimizations that can improve battery performance. Go to Settings > Software Update to check for the latest system updates, and update your apps via the Google Play Store.

Consult Samsung Support

If none of these steps resolve the issue, it's a good idea to consult Samsung Support. They can provide further troubleshooting advice or direct you to a service center if the issue requires professional assistance.

By following these steps, you can troubleshoot and resolve most battery-related issues, ensuring your Galaxy S25 Ultra performs at its best.

Understanding AI Power Management for Smarter Use

The Galaxy S25 Ultra is equipped with advanced AI features that intelligently manage power consumption, helping you get the most out of your battery without any extra effort. Here's how these AI-driven features work to enhance battery efficiency and prolong usage time.

Personal Data Engine

The Personal Data Engine uses on-device AI to analyze your usage patterns. Based on this analysis, it automatically adjusts settings to optimize battery performance. For example, if you tend to use certain apps at specific times of the day, the AI will ensure these apps get the resources they need while reducing power to less frequently used apps.

Adaptive Battery

Adaptive Battery learns which apps you use most frequently and prioritizes them by providing more power when needed. It reduces power to apps that aren't used often, preventing them from draining your battery unnecessarily. Over time, the AI gets better at predicting your habits, helping you conserve energy throughout the day.

App Power Monitor

The App Power Monitor tracks apps that consume excessive battery power and suggests actions you can take to reduce their impact. Whether it's limiting background activity or recommending settings adjustments, this feature helps you keep track of battery-draining apps and take action before they affect your battery life.

Dynamic Power Allocation

AI-powered Dynamic Power Allocation adjusts the performance of your device's CPU and GPU based on your usage. For demanding tasks like gaming or video editing, the system allocates more resources, while for simpler tasks like texting or browsing, it reduces power consumption. This ensures you get maximum performance when needed, without wasting energy on less intensive tasks.

AI-Driven Charging Management

The device learns your charging habits, such as typically charging overnight, and delays reaching a full charge until just before you usually unplug it. This reduces the time the battery spends at 100%, which helps preserve its long-term health by minimizing stress on the battery.

Power-Aware Camera Settings

When your battery is running low, the AI automatically adjusts camera settings to conserve power. It may reduce the camera's resolution or disable certain features to extend battery life, so you can still capture moments even when your device is low on power.

Smart Device Integration

AI also allows your Galaxy S25 Ultra to communicate with other connected devices, such as your smartwatch or earbuds, to sync power settings across your ecosystem. When not in use, all devices are optimized for battery conservation, ensuring maximum efficiency across the board.

By leveraging these AI features, your device intelligently manages power consumption, ensuring that your Galaxy S25 Ultra lasts longer without requiring you to manually adjust settings.

Chapter 5

Security and Privacy

Biometric Security: Fingerprint, Face Recognition, and More

Your Galaxy S25 Ultra offers advanced biometric security options to keep your device and data safe while ensuring easy access. Let's explore the different methods for unlocking your device and securing sensitive information.

Fingerprint Recognition

The in-screen ultrasonic fingerprint sensor provides quick and secure access to your device. To set it up, go to Settings > Biometrics and Security > Fingerprints. Follow the on-screen instructions to register your fingerprint. The sensor works by scanning the unique patterns in your fingerprint, allowing you to unlock your phone with a simple touch. This method ensures high security while being fast and convenient.

Facial Recognition

Facial recognition is another great way to unlock your device. It uses advanced AI algorithms to map your face for secure access. To enable facial recognition, navigate to Settings > Biometrics and Security > Face Recognition and follow the setup process. The device uses your facial features to recognize you and unlock the phone in seconds. It's a fast, hands-free way to secure your phone without needing to touch anything.

Enhanced Security Measures

For added security, you can activate features like "Identity Check", which requires biometric authentication to access sensitive settings and apps. To enable this feature, go to Settings > Biometrics and Security and look for options that allow you to lock down apps, settings, or specific features. This adds an extra layer of protection against unauthorized access, ensuring that even if someone gains physical access to your device, they can't unlock sensitive areas without your biometric information.

These biometric options give you a seamless and secure experience, making it easier to access your device while keeping your personal data safe. Whether you prefer fingerprint recognition, facial scanning, or both, your Galaxy S25 Ultra offers top-tier security features that are both effective and convenient.

Using Secure Folders and Privacy Controls

Your Galaxy S25 Ultra provides powerful tools to safeguard your sensitive information. By using features like Secure Folder and adjusting your privacy settings, you can ensure that your personal data remains protected. Here's how to make the most of these privacy features:

Secure Folder

Secure Folder is an encrypted space on your device where you can store apps, files, and data that you want to keep private. To set it up, go to Settings > Biometrics and Security > Secure Folder. Once activated, you can move apps and files into the folder, ensuring that they are protected by a separate password, PIN, or biometric authentication. This feature is great for keeping sensitive apps, like banking or personal documents, away from prying eyes.

Privacy Dashboard

The Privacy Dashboard lets you monitor and manage app permissions, ensuring that only authorized apps can access your personal information, such as your location, contacts, or camera. To access the Privacy Dashboard, go to Settings > Privacy > Privacy Dashboard. Here, you can see which apps have accessed sensitive data and adjust permissions accordingly. If an app doesn't need certain permissions, you can revoke them to further protect your privacy.

Data Encryption

Enabling full-device encryption ensures that all your data is protected from unauthorized access, especially in the event that your device is lost or stolen. To turn on encryption, go to Settings > Biometrics and Security > Encrypt Device. Once enabled, your data will be securely locked and inaccessible without your password or biometric authentication, providing peace of mind that your information is safe.

By using Secure Folder, the Privacy Dashboard, and data encryption, you can take control of your device's security and protect your personal information. These tools empower you to safeguard your privacy with ease, ensuring your Galaxy S25 Ultra remains a secure space for your data.

Managing App Permissions and Data Sharing

Your Galaxy S25 Ultra provides powerful tools for managing app permissions and data sharing, giving you control over how your personal information is accessed and used. Here's how to take charge of your app settings and ensure your privacy is protected.

App Permission Management

Each app on your device requests certain permissions, such as access to your location, camera, or contacts. You can review and adjust these permissions at any time to limit access to sensitive features. To manage permissions, go to Settings > Apps > [App Name] > Permissions. From here, you can allow or deny individual permissions for each app. For example, if an app doesn't need access to your camera, you can disable this permission to enhance privacy.

Data Sharing Preferences

Many apps and services share your data with third-party services for advertising or analytics purposes. You can set preferences to control how your information is shared. To adjust data sharing settings, go to Settings > Privacy > Permissions Manager or check specific app settings for privacy and data-sharing options. Limiting the amount of data shared with third parties ensures that only necessary information is exposed, keeping your personal details more secure.

Background Data Restrictions

Apps may use data in the background even when you're not actively using them. This can drain your battery and expose you to unnecessary data collection. To prevent apps from using data without your consent, go to Settings > Connections > Data Usage and enable Restrict Background Data for individual apps. This ensures that apps only use data when they are actively being used, helping to conserve battery life and protect your privacy.

By managing app permissions, controlling data sharing preferences, and restricting background data, you can ensure that your personal information is used according to your preferences. These simple steps help you maintain greater control over your privacy while optimizing your device's performance.

How to Locate a Lost Device with Samsung Find My Mobile

Losing your Galaxy S25 Ultra can be stressful, but with Samsung's Find My Mobile service, you can quickly locate your device, lock it to prevent unauthorized access, or even erase your personal data for added security. Here's how to set it up and use it if your device is lost.

Setting Up Find My Mobile

To use Find My Mobile, you need to make sure the service is activated on your device. Start by signing into your Samsung account on your Galaxy S25 Ultra. Next, enable location services and activate Find My Mobile by going to Settings > Biometrics and Security > Find My Mobile. Toggle the setting to On and ensure that both Remote Unlock and Send Last Location are enabled. This will allow Samsung to locate your device even if the battery is low or the device is turned off.

Locating Your Device

If your device goes missing, you can use Find My Mobile to track its location. Simply go to the Find My Mobile website (findmymobile.samsung.com) or use the Find My Mobile app on another device. Sign in with your Samsung account, and you'll be able to view your device's current location on a map. If your device is nearby, you can also use the "Ring" feature to make it emit a sound, helping you find it.

Remote Lock and Erase

If your device is lost or stolen, Find My Mobile lets you remotely lock your device to prevent unauthorized access. To do this, select Lock from the Find My Mobile interface, and you can also add a message or contact number for the person who finds your device. If you're concerned about the security of your data, you can use the Erase Data option to remotely wipe all of your personal information from the device. This ensures that your data remains secure, even if your phone cannot be recovered.

By setting up Find My Mobile, you ensure that you have the tools you need to locate, lock, and protect your device in case it gets lost. These features offer peace of mind, knowing that your personal data is secure and you have the option to recover or protect your device.

Chapter 6

Multitasking and Advanced Features

Samsung DeX: Transforming Your Phone into a Desktop

Samsung DeX allows you to turn your Galaxy S25 Ultra into a full-fledged desktop computer, enhancing your productivity whether you're at home, at the office, or on the go. Here's how to make the most of this powerful feature.

Connecting to External Displays

To get started with Samsung DeX, connect your Galaxy S25 Ultra to an external display. You can use a USB-C to HDMI cable to link your phone to a monitor or TV. Alternatively, if you have a compatible smart TV or monitor, you can connect wirelessly. Once connected, you'll be able to expand your workspace and manage multiple tasks at once with a larger screen.

Desktop-Like Interface

Once your device is connected to an external display, you'll be greeted with a desktop-like interface. This includes a taskbar, resizable windows, and support for both mouse and keyboard input, making navigation and multitasking smooth and efficient. The interface is designed to resemble the familiar desktop experience, allowing you to work as if you were on a traditional computer.

App Compatibility

Samsung DeX supports running mobile apps in a desktop format, so you can seamlessly switch between tasks like document editing, web browsing, and media consumption without the need for separate devices. Apps will open in resizable windows, and you can use them just like you would on a PC or laptop, boosting your efficiency.

Wireless DeX

For a more clutter-free experience, Wireless DeX allows you to connect your device wirelessly to supported smart TVs or monitors. This eliminates the need for physical cables, giving you more flexibility to set up your workspace wherever you go. Simply ensure that both your phone and the display are on the same Wi-Fi network, and you'll be ready to go.

Peripheral Support

To further enhance your desktop experience, you can connect peripherals such as a mouse, keyboard, or external storage devices. This transforms your Galaxy S25 Ultra into a portable workstation, allowing you to work efficiently no matter where you are.

By using Samsung DeX, you can transform your Galaxy S25 Ultra into a powerful desktop replacement, offering flexibility and productivity on the go. Whether you're working on documents or enjoying media, DeX gives you the versatility of a desktop experience from your mobile device.

Using Split-Screen and App Pairing for Efficient Multitasking

Your Galaxy S25 Ultra offers several multitasking features that allow you to work efficiently and switch between tasks seamlessly. Here's how to take full advantage of split-screen and app pairing to boost your productivity.

Activating Split-Screen Mode

Split-screen mode lets you view two apps simultaneously, making it easy to multitask. To activate this feature:

1. Open the recent apps screen by tapping the Recents button.
2. Find the app you want to use and tap the three dots at the top of the app's preview.
3. Select "Open in split-screen view".
4. Then, choose a second app from your app list, and it will appear in the lower window. You can now use both apps at the same time, whether you're browsing the web while checking emails or using a notes app alongside a document.

App Pairing

App Pairing allows you to create shortcuts for app combinations you use frequently, making it easy to launch them together with a single tap. To create an App Pair:

1. Open the Edge Panel by swiping from the edge of the screen.
2. Tap "Create App Pair" and select two apps you often use together.
3. Once created, you can access this pair from the Edge Panel anytime, launching both apps in split-screen mode instantly. This feature saves time by eliminating the need to open each app separately.

Adjusting Window Sizes

You can resize the windows in split-screen mode to optimize your screen space. Simply drag the divider between the two apps to adjust the size of each window according to your needs. This allows you to prioritize one app or split the screen equally for multitasking.

Using Pop-Up View

If you need even more flexibility, try Pop-Up View. This feature lets you open apps in resizable windows that you can move around the screen. To use Pop-Up View:

1. Open an app, then tap the three dots in the top-right corner of the app window.
2. Select "Open in pop-up view". The app will open in a floating window, allowing you to manage multiple tasks without the clutter of multiple screens.

Edge Panel Integration

The Edge Panel makes multitasking even easier. Use it to quickly access apps and launch them directly in split-screen or pop-up view, streamlining your workflow and reducing the time spent switching between apps.

By utilizing split-screen, app pairing, and pop-up view, you can efficiently multitask and manage multiple tasks on your Galaxy S25 Ultra, boosting your productivity and making your device more versatile for your daily needs.

Mastering Samsung Bixby: The Voice Assistant that Does It All

Samsung's Bixby is a powerful voice assistant that can make your Galaxy S25 Ultra even more efficient. With Bixby, you can perform tasks, control smart devices, and automate routines using just your voice. Here's how to make the most of it.

Voice Commands

Activate Bixby simply by saying, "Hi Bixby," or pressing the dedicated Bixby button. Once it's listening, issue commands like:

- "Set an alarm for 7 AM."
- "Send a message to John."
- "What's the weather today?" Bixby can handle a wide range of tasks, from setting reminders to sending texts, all without you needing to touch the screen.

Bixby Vision

With Bixby Vision, your phone's camera becomes a tool for identifying objects, translating text, and even shopping online. Just point your camera at an item or text, and Bixby can:

- Identify the object and provide more information.
- Translate text when you're traveling abroad or need quick translations.
- Find products online based on the item you're looking at. This feature makes it easy to get things done faster and smarter.

Routine Automation

Bixby can help you automate daily tasks with Routine Automation. For example, you can create a custom routine triggered by a simple command like "Good morning." Bixby will then:

- Turn on your lights.
- Read out the weather.
- Start your favorite playlist. This feature saves you time and simplifies your daily activities, all with a single voice command.

Bixby on Other Devices

Bixby isn't just for your phone. You can use it to control compatible smart home devices, such as lights, thermostats, and smart appliances. Simply say, "Hi Bixby, turn on the lights," and Bixby will handle the rest. This integration makes it easy to manage your home's smart ecosystem directly from your Galaxy S25 Ultra.

AI Enhancements

Bixby gets smarter over time. With its AI capabilities, it learns your preferences and habits, allowing it to provide personalized responses. The more you interact with Bixby, the more it adapts to your needs, offering a more natural and tailored experience.

By mastering Bixby, you'll make your Galaxy S25 Ultra more intuitive and efficient, turning everyday tasks into quick, hands-free actions.

Exploring Hidden Features and Developer Options

Your Galaxy S25 Ultra comes with hidden features and advanced settings that can be unlocked through the Developer Options. These options provide tools that allow you to customize your device and enhance its performance. Here's how to access them and what they can do for you.

Enabling Developer Options

To unlock the Developer Options menu, go to Settings > About phone > Software information, and tap the Build number seven times. This will activate Developer Options in the Settings menu. While designed primarily for developers, these settings offer useful tools for power users looking to get more out of their device.

USB Debugging

USB debugging is a powerful feature that allows you to connect your Galaxy S25 Ultra to a computer for advanced interactions, like transferring large files, testing apps, or using ADB (Android Debug Bridge) commands. This feature is particularly useful for troubleshooting or when you need additional control over your device during development or debugging.

Animation Scale Adjustments

In Developer Options, you can adjust or even disable window and transition animations, which can make your device feel faster and more responsive. To do this, navigate to Settings > Developer Options and adjust the Window animation scale, Transition animation scale, and Animator duration scale. Lowering or turning off these animations can improve the user experience, especially on older devices, by speeding up interactions.

Force GPU Rendering

Enabling Force GPU rendering ensures that tasks typically handled by the CPU are instead rendered by the Graphics Processing Unit (GPU). This can lead to smoother graphics and enhanced performance, particularly in gaming or media-intensive apps. To enable it, go to Developer Options and toggle on Force GPU rendering for better visual performance.

Background Process Limit

You can limit the number of processes that run in the background by setting a cap in the Developer Options. By limiting background processes, you can save battery and reduce the system load, especially if your device is running slow. However, be mindful that this may affect the performance of some apps. Find this option in Developer Options > Limit background processes.

Strict Mode

Enable Strict Mode to highlight apps that are not optimized for smooth performance. This feature detects long-running operations that can cause lag, giving you a visual indicator of apps that may need attention. To enable it, go to Developer Options and toggle on Strict Mode for better performance monitoring.

Network Speed Display

Network speed display shows real-time data speeds in the status bar, which can help you monitor your connectivity performance. This is especially useful when you need to troubleshoot slow internet connections or track data usage during heavy downloads or live streaming. Enable this feature in Developer Options > Show network speed.

By using these Developer Options, you can enhance your device's performance, customize settings, and optimize your Galaxy S25 Ultra for a smoother, more responsive experience. Whether you're a developer or a power user, these features allow you to unlock the full potential of your device.

Chapter 7

Connectivity and Smart Device Integration

Setting Up Wi-Fi, Bluetooth, and 5G Connectivity

Setting up Wi-Fi, Bluetooth, and 5G on your Galaxy S25 Ultra is straightforward and ensures that you can stay connected with ease. Here's how to configure each of these features to get the best performance from your device.

Wi-Fi Setup

1. Open Settings and navigate to Connections > Wi-Fi.
2. Toggle the switch to On to enable Wi-Fi.
3. Select your preferred Wi-Fi network from the list of available options.
4. If the network is secured, enter the password provided by the network administrator.

For quick sharing of your Wi-Fi credentials, tap the QR code icon next to the network name, which allows others to scan and connect without needing to enter a password manually.

Bluetooth Pairing

1. Go to Settings > Connections > Bluetooth and toggle it to On.
2. Make sure your Bluetooth device is in pairing mode (refer to the device's manual if unsure).
3. Your device will scan for nearby Bluetooth devices. Once your device appears in the list, tap to select it.
4. If required, enter the PIN or passcode provided by the Bluetooth device to complete the pairing process.

Once paired, your Bluetooth device should automatically connect whenever both devices are within range.

5G Configuration

1. Go to Settings > Connections > Mobile networks > Network mode.
2. Select 5G/LTE/3G/2G auto connect to enable 5G connectivity.

Ensure your carrier supports 5G services and that you are in a 5G coverage area for the best speeds. With 5G enabled, you'll enjoy faster download speeds, lower latency, and improved overall network performance when available.

By following these simple steps, you'll be able to set up Wi-Fi, Bluetooth, and 5G connectivity on your Galaxy S25 Ultra and experience seamless connectivity for all your needs.

Connecting to Other Samsung Devices: SmartThings, Wearables, and More

Your Galaxy S25 Ultra is designed to work seamlessly with other Samsung devices, creating a connected ecosystem that enhances your everyday experience. Whether you're integrating smart home devices, pairing with wearables, or using Samsung DeX, here's how to set up each feature.

SmartThings Integration

Samsung's SmartThings app allows you to control and monitor a variety of smart home devices directly from your phone. To get started:

1. Install the SmartThings app from the Galaxy Store or Google Play.
2. Open the app and sign in with your Samsung account.
3. Tap the "+" icon to add devices.
4. Follow the on-screen instructions to connect compatible devices, such as lights, thermostats, and cameras. Once set up, you can control your devices from your phone or automate them to fit your lifestyle.

Wearable Pairing

Connecting wearables like the Galaxy Watch or Galaxy Buds to your Galaxy S25 Ultra is simple:

1. Ensure Bluetooth is enabled on your phone by going to Settings > Connections > Bluetooth.

2. Open the respective app, such as Galaxy Wearable for watches or Galaxy Buds for earphones.
3. Follow the prompts in the app to pair your device. Make sure your wearable is in pairing mode and close to the phone. Once paired, you can easily access features like notifications, fitness tracking, and music controls.

Samsung DeX Connection

Samsung DeX turns your Galaxy S25 Ultra into a desktop-like experience, perfect for multitasking or working on the go. To use DeX:

1. Connect your phone to a compatible monitor using a USB-C to HDMI cable, or wirelessly to a supported smart TV.
2. Follow the on-screen instructions to enable DeX mode. DeX gives you a familiar desktop interface with access to apps, a taskbar, and resizable windows, turning your phone into a portable workstation.

By setting up SmartThings, pairing with your wearables, and using Samsung DeX, you can create a fully integrated Samsung ecosystem that works together seamlessly, making your Galaxy S25 Ultra even more powerful and versatile.

How to Optimize Your Galaxy S25 Ultra for Maximum Speed

To ensure that your Galaxy S25 Ultra is performing at its best, optimizing your connectivity can lead to faster and more reliable connections. Here's how to fine-tune various settings for maximum speed:

Network Mode Settings

Adjusting your Network mode ensures you get the best possible connection depending on your carrier's capabilities and your location.

1. Go to Settings > Connections > Mobile networks > Network mode.
2. Select 5G/LTE/3G/2G auto connect for the most consistent speeds, especially if you're in a 5G coverage area.
   This setting will automatically switch between 5G, LTE, and other networks for optimal performance based on signal strength.

Wi-Fi Optimization

To improve Wi-Fi speeds, follow these steps:

1. Use a Wi-Fi analyzer tool (available in the Galaxy Store or third-party apps) to identify less congested channels and avoid interference.
2. Connect to 5GHz networks when possible, as they tend to offer faster speeds than 2.4GHz networks.
3. Ensure your router's firmware is up to date for the latest performance improvements.
4. Place the router in a central location in your home to minimize interference and dead zones, ensuring a more stable and faster connection.

Bluetooth Performance

For stable Bluetooth connections, ensure your device is within an optimal range of the connected device. Avoid placing your phone between the Bluetooth device and any obstacles, as this can weaken the signal. Keeping devices within a reasonable distance will help maintain a strong, uninterrupted connection.

Software Updates

Software updates often include performance optimizations and bug fixes that improve connectivity and overall device performance. To stay up-to-date:

1. Go to Settings > Software update > Download and install.
2. Regularly check for updates to ensure your device is running the latest improvements and enhancements.

By following these simple strategies—adjusting network modes, optimizing Wi-Fi settings, ensuring Bluetooth stability, and keeping your device updated—you'll ensure your Galaxy S25 Ultra runs smoothly, providing the best possible speed and connectivity.

Troubleshooting Connectivity Issues

If you're experiencing connectivity issues with your Galaxy S25 Ultra, there are several simple troubleshooting steps you can take to resolve common problems. Follow these steps to quickly fix issues with Wi-Fi, Bluetooth, or mobile data.

Reboot the Device

A quick reboot can often resolve temporary connectivity issues by refreshing the network settings.

1. Power off your device.
2. Wait for about 30 seconds.
3. Power it back on.
   This can help restore stable connections and refresh your network settings.

Reset Network Settings

If issues persist, try resetting all network-related settings to their default configurations. This will reset Wi-Fi, Bluetooth, and mobile data settings.

1. Go to Settings > General management > Reset.
2. Tap Reset network settings and confirm.
   This step can resolve deeper network configuration issues.

Toggle Airplane Mode

Activate and deactivate Airplane Mode to reset network connections without rebooting your device.

1. Swipe down to open the Quick Settings panel.
2. Tap the Airplane Mode icon to activate it.
3. Wait about 10 seconds and then deactivate it.
   This can help resolve minor issues with Wi-Fi, Bluetooth, or cellular connections by refreshing the network interfaces.

Check for Interference

Physical obstructions or electronic interference can affect your network connections. For **Wi-Fi**, check for thick walls, metal objects, or appliances like microwaves that might weaken the signal. For Bluetooth, ensure there are no other devices causing interference by operating on the same frequency.

Update Router Firmware

For Wi-Fi issues, check if your router's firmware is up to date. Manufacturers often release updates to improve performance and security.

1. Log in to your router's settings page (usually accessible via a browser).

2. Check for any firmware updates and install them.
3. Make sure your router is operating on the least congested Wi-Fi channel, especially if you're in an area with many nearby networks.

Clear Cache and Data for Problematic Apps

If a specific app is causing connectivity problems, clearing its cache or data may resolve the issue.

1. Go to Settings > Apps > [App Name] > Storage.
2. Tap Clear Cache or Clear Data to resolve app-specific connectivity problems.

Contact Your Service Provider

If these steps don't fix the issue, contact your mobile or internet service provider. They can check for network outages, signal disruptions, or service limitations in your area and may offer additional troubleshooting tips tailored to your network.

By following these troubleshooting steps, you can quickly resolve common connectivity issues and ensure a smooth and reliable experience on your Galaxy S25 Ultra.

Chapter 8

Storage and Data Management

Managing storage is essential to ensure your device runs smoothly. Here's how you can easily free up space on your device and make use of cloud services to manage your data efficiently.

Freeing Up Storage

1. **Navigate to Storage Settings**
   Start by going to *Settings > Battery and device care > Storage*. This will give you an overview of how your storage is being used.

2. **Review Categories**
   You'll see categories like *Images*, *Videos*, and *Apps*. Tap on each category to see how much space is being used. This will help you identify areas where you can free up space.

3. **Delete Unneeded Files**
   For images and videos you no longer need, simply select them and hit delete. If you have apps you rarely use, uninstall them to free up storage.

4. **Use the 'Clean Now' Feature**
   Samsung devices offer a convenient *"Clean now"* feature that helps remove residual files, like cache and leftover app data, that take up unnecessary space. Make sure to use this tool regularly to maintain a clean device.

Utilizing Cloud Services

1. **Enable Cloud Backups**
   Set up automatic backups with Samsung Cloud or Google Drive to keep your photos, videos, and documents safe without using up your device's storage. You can do this by navigating to *Settings > Accounts and backup* and selecting *Backup and restore*.

2. **Transfer Files to Cloud Storage**
   For photos, videos, and documents that you don't need immediately, transfer them to cloud storage to free up local space. Google Drive and Samsung Cloud both offer plenty of storage space for your essential files.

3. **Explore Third-Party Services**
   For additional storage, consider using services like Microsoft OneDrive, which provides extra cloud storage and syncs seamlessly across devices.

By following these steps, you can easily free up space on your device and keep your files organized with cloud backups, ensuring that your device remains fast and efficient.

Best Practices for Backing Up Your Data and Restoring it When Needed

Backing up your data is crucial for protecting against accidental loss. Here's how you can back up your data using Samsung Cloud and Google Drive, and restore it when necessary, ensuring that your important files are always safe.

Samsung Cloud Backup

1. **Navigate to Samsung Cloud Settings**
   Go to *Settings > Accounts and backup > Samsung Cloud* to begin the backup process.

2. **Select Data to Back Up**
   Tap *Back up data* and choose which items you want to back up, such as photos, contacts, apps, and settings.

3. **Enable Automatic Backups**
   For added convenience, enable *Auto back up while roaming* under settings. This ensures that your device automatically backs up your data, even when you're not on Wi-Fi.

Google Drive Backup

1. **Access Google Drive Backup Settings**
   Navigate to *Settings > Accounts and backup > Google Drive* to manage your Google Drive backup.

2. **Perform a Manual Backup**
   Tap *Back up now* to initiate a manual backup. This is a great option if you want to ensure your data is up to date immediately.
3. **Enable Automatic Backups**
   To back up data automatically, make sure *Back up using mobile or metered Wi-Fi data* is enabled. This will keep your data secure, even when you're not on a Wi-Fi network.

Restoring Data

1. **Restore from Samsung Cloud**
   To restore data from Samsung Cloud, go to *Settings > Accounts and backup > Restore data*. Choose the backup you want to restore from and select the data to bring back to your device.
2. **Restore from Google Drive**
   For Google Drive, sign in to your Google account and follow the prompts to restore your data. Your apps, contacts, photos, and other files will be seamlessly restored to your device.

By following these simple steps, you'll ensure that your data is always backed up and can be easily restored whenever needed, giving you peace of mind and preventing data loss.

File Management Tips for Photos, Videos, and Documents

Efficient file management helps you stay organized and ensures that your important media and documents are easy to access. Here's how you can manage your photos, videos, and documents effectively.

Using My Files App

- **Access All Your Files**: Open the *My Files* app to view all the files stored on your device.
- **Organize Files**: Create folders for different categories of files (e.g., work, personal, media) to keep everything in order.
- **Search Function**: Use the search bar to quickly locate specific files when you need them.

Managing Photos and Videos

- **Gallery App**: Use the *Gallery* app to view, organize, and edit your photos and videos.
- **Create Albums**: Organize your media by creating albums based on themes (e.g., vacations, family, events).
- **Recover Deleted Items**: If you accidentally delete something, check the *Trash* feature. You can restore deleted photos or videos within 30 days.

Document Organization

- **Store Documents in the Documents Folder**: Keep your documents organized in the *Documents* folder within *My Files* for easy access.
- **Use Cloud Services**: For additional storage and seamless access across devices, use cloud services like Google Drive. This also ensures that your documents are backed up.
- **Regular Backups**: Back up important documents regularly to avoid the risk of data loss.

By following these simple steps, you can easily organize and manage your files, ensuring that your photos, videos, and documents are accessible and secure.

Managing App Data and Using External Storage Devices

Managing app data and utilizing external storage devices effectively can help you free up space and keep your device running smoothly. Here's how to do both.

Managing App Data

1. **Access Installed Apps**: Go to *Settings > Apps* to view all the apps installed on your device.
2. **Check Data Usage**: Select an app to see its storage usage and how much space its data is taking up.
3. **Free Up Space**: Tap on *Clear cache* to remove temporary files and *Clear data* to reset the app and remove all stored data. Be mindful, clearing data will log you out of the app, and you'll lose any saved settings.

Using External Storage Devices

1. **Connect via USB-C**: Use a USB-C cable with the appropriate adapter to connect external storage devices, such as flash drives or external hard drives, to your device.
2. **Transfer Files**: Open the *My Files* app to access both your device storage and external storage. You can easily transfer files between the two by selecting the files you want to move and choosing the destination.
3. **Exercise Caution**: Always double-check before moving or deleting files on your external storage device. Accidental data loss is possible, so make sure your files are properly backed up before making any changes.

By following these practical steps, you can effectively manage your app data and expand your storage options using external devices, ensuring your device remains optimized and clutter-free.

Chapter 9

Personalizing Your Device

Customizing Your Home Screen: Themes, Widgets, and App Layouts

Customizing your home screen not only gives your device a personal touch but also boosts your productivity by organizing everything just the way you like it. Here's how to transform your home screen into a space that works for you.

Applying Themes

1. **Access Themes**: Open the *Settings* app, then navigate to *Themes*.
2. **Browse Available Themes**: You'll find a selection of pre-installed themes. You can also explore the *Theme Store* to download new themes that match your style or mood.
3. **Apply Your Theme**: Once you've found the perfect theme, simply select it. This will automatically change your icons, wallpapers, and system colors to match the chosen theme.

Adding and Customizing Widgets

1. **Add Widgets to Your Home Screen**: Long-press an empty area on your home screen and select *Widgets* from the menu.
2. **Place and Resize Widgets**: Choose the widget you want to add, drag it to your desired location, and resize it if necessary by dragging the edges.
3. **Customize Widget Settings**: To make the widget work exactly how you want, tap on it to access its settings and adjust the options to suit your preferences.

Organizing App Layouts

1. **Create Folders**: To keep your apps organized, drag one app icon over another to create a folder.
2. **Rename Folders**: Tap on the folder name and rename it to reflect the categories of apps inside, such as *Work*, *Social*, or *Utilities*.

3. **Arrange Apps for Easy Access**: Organize your apps by frequency of use or priority. Place your most-used apps in easy-to-reach spots for quicker access.

By following these simple steps, you'll not only make your device look great, but you'll also create a workspace that makes it easier to access your favorite apps and stay productive.

Setting Ringtones, Notifications, and Alerts

Customizing your device's sound settings not only helps you personalize your experience but also ensures that you never miss an important call, message, or notification. Here's how to tailor your sound settings to fit your preferences.

Changing Ringtones

1. **Access Ringtone Settings**: Go to *Settings > Sound & vibration > Ringtone*.
2. **Choose a Ringtone**: From the list of available ringtones, select the one that suits your style. You can tap on each option to hear a preview.
3. **Set a Custom Ringtone**: If you prefer a unique sound, tap *Add* to choose a custom audio file from your device. This could be a favorite song or a recording.

Customizing Notification Sounds

1. **Navigate to App Notification Settings**: Go to *Settings > Apps > [App Name] > Notifications*.
2. **Select Notification Categories**: Choose a specific notification category (e.g., Messages, Email, Alerts).
3. **Pick Your Tone**: Tap on *Sound* to select a different notification tone for each category, ensuring that each type of alert has a distinct sound.

Adjusting Alert Settings

1. **Personalize Sound & Vibration**: In *Sound & vibration*, you can adjust the intensity of vibrations, set *Do Not Disturb* to limit interruptions, and customize Emergency alerts to make sure you're always aware of important notifications.
2. **Advanced Audio Controls**: For more fine-tuned control, use *Sound Assistant* (available through Samsung's *Good Lock* app). This feature lets you set different volumes for each app and provides shortcuts for managing playback.

By adjusting these settings, you'll create a sound experience that's not only personalized but also efficient, helping you stay on top of your alerts without being overwhelmed.

Adjusting System Preferences for Comfort: Dark Mode, Display, and Accessibility

Adjusting your device's settings for comfort and accessibility ensures that you have a user-friendly experience tailored to your preferences. Here's how you can optimize your device to meet your needs.

Enabling Dark Mode

1. **Open Display Settings**: Go to *Settings > Display*.
2. **Activate Dark Theme**: Toggle on *Dark theme*. This setting reduces eye strain, especially in low-light environments, and also helps conserve battery life on OLED screens.

Customizing Display Settings

1. **Adjust Brightness**: In the *Display* section, use the *Brightness* slider to set the level that's most comfortable for your eyes.
2. **Set Screen Timeout**: Choose how long your device's screen will stay on when idle by adjusting the *Screen timeout* setting. This helps save battery while maintaining usability.
3. **Font Size and Style**: Modify the *Font size* and *Font style* to suit your preferences. Larger fonts can make reading easier, while different styles can add a personal touch to your display.
4. **Enable Adaptive Brightness**: Turn on *Adaptive brightness* to automatically adjust the screen brightness based on the lighting around you, providing optimal viewing in various environments.

Enhancing Accessibility

1. **Access Accessibility Settings**: Go to *Settings > Accessibility* to explore features that improve usability.
2. **Enable Magnification Gestures**: Activate *Magnification gestures* for the ability to zoom in on specific parts of the screen for a closer look.

3. **Use Color Inversion**: If you find standard color schemes challenging, turn on *Color inversion* to switch to high-contrast colors for better visibility.

4. **Enable TalkBack**: *TalkBack* provides spoken feedback to help navigate your device. It's especially useful for users with visual impairments.

5. **Quick Access Shortcuts**: Set up *Accessibility shortcuts* to easily access your most frequently used features, like magnification or TalkBack, with a simple gesture or button press.

By adjusting these settings, you can make your device more comfortable and accessible, ensuring a personalized experience that works best for you.

Managing Notifications and Quick Settings for Efficiency

Streamlining your notifications and quick settings will help you stay organized and access important features quickly. Here's how you can optimize both to boost efficiency.

Customizing Quick Settings

1. **Access Quick Settings**: Swipe down from the top of the screen to open the *Quick Settings* panel.

2. **Edit Quick Settings**: Tap *Edit* to rearrange the tiles. You can add, remove, or move features like Wi-Fi, Bluetooth, and *Do Not Disturb* to make the panel more suited to your needs.

Managing Notifications

1. **Access Notification Settings**: Go to *Settings > Notifications* to manage how your device alerts you.

2. **Advanced Settings**: Use the *Advanced settings* to activate features like *Snooze notifications*, *Notification history*, and *App icon badges* to ensure you never miss an important alert.

Optimizing Notification Categories

1. **Customize App Notifications**: In *Settings > Notifications*, you can customize notification categories for each app. For example, select whether you want to receive *promotions*, *updates*, or only *critical alerts*, and adjust their priority. This allows you to focus on the notifications that matter most.

Mute or Silence Notifications

1. **Use Do Not Disturb Mode**: Activate *Do Not Disturb* to silence notifications temporarily during meetings or while sleeping. You can also customize the settings to allow certain contacts or apps to bypass the silence, ensuring you stay updated on what's important.

Customizing Notification Sounds and Vibration

1. **Set Custom Sounds or Vibration**: For apps or contacts that matter most, assign custom notification sounds or vibrations. This way, you can easily identify urgent messages or reminders without checking your phone.

Using Notification Channels

1. **Organize Notifications by Channel**: Some apps allow you to organize notifications into channels. For example, you can choose to receive *promotional emails* silently while ensuring that *messages or calls* alert you with sound.

By streamlining these settings, you can enhance your device's efficiency, ensuring that important notifications are easy to access while minimizing distractions.

Chapter 10

Troubleshooting, Maintenance, and Support

Solving Common Galaxy S25 Ultra Problems

The Galaxy S25 Ultra is a powerful device, but like any smartphone, it may occasionally encounter issues. Here's how you can quickly identify and resolve some of the most common problems to keep your device running smoothly.

Overheating During Intensive Use

- **What to do**: If your device becomes warm during activities like gaming or video recording, it's typically normal. However, if it overheats:
  - Close unused apps running in the background.
  - Lower the screen brightness.
  - Use the device in a cooler environment.

Battery Draining Faster Than Expected

- **What to do**: To help extend battery life:
  - Disable features like Bluetooth and GPS when not in use.
  - Reduce the screen timeout setting.
  - Go to *Settings* > *Battery* to check which apps are consuming excessive power, and consider closing or uninstalling them.

App Crashes or Freezes

- **What to do**: If an app frequently crashes or freezes:
  - Go to *Settings* > *Apps* > [App Name] > *Storage* > *Clear Cache*.
  - If the issue persists, try reinstalling the app to eliminate any corrupted data.

Connectivity Issues (Wi-Fi/Bluetooth)

- **What to do**: For Wi-Fi or Bluetooth connectivity problems:

- ○ Toggle *Airplane Mode* on and off to reset connections.
- ○ Restart your router or Bluetooth device.
- ○ Ensure your device's software is up to date in *Settings > Software update*.

Camera Performance Problems

- • **What to do**: If your camera isn't working as expected:
  - ○ Ensure the lens is clean and free from obstructions.
  - ○ Restart the camera app.
  - ○ If issues persist, try performing a soft reset of the device by restarting it.

By following these simple solutions, you can resolve many common Galaxy S25 Ultra problems and keep your device performing at its best.

How to Perform a Factory Reset Safely

Performing a factory reset can resolve persistent issues with your device, but it's important to ensure that your data is backed up and that the reset process is done correctly. Follow these steps to safely reset your Galaxy S25 Ultra.

Preparation
Before you reset your device, take these steps to safeguard your data:

1. **Back Up Important Data**: Use Samsung Cloud, Google Drive, or an external storage device to back up your important files, photos, and apps.
2. **Remove External SD Cards or SIM Cards**: To prevent potential data loss, remove any external SD cards or SIM cards from your device.

Factory Reset via Settings

1. **Open Settings**: Navigate to *Settings > General management > Reset > Factory data reset*.
2. **Review the Information**: Carefully read the information provided about the reset. This will let you know what data will be erased.
3. **Tap Reset**: Tap the *Reset* button to begin the process.
4. **Enter Your Credentials**: If prompted, enter your credentials (PIN, pattern, or password).

5. **Delete All**: Confirm the reset by tapping *Delete all*. This will erase all data from your device, returning it to its factory settings.

Factory Reset via Recovery Mode (if device is unresponsive)

If your device isn't responding, you can perform a reset through recovery mode:

1. **Power Off Your Device**: Turn off your Galaxy S25 Ultra completely.
2. **Enter Recovery Mode**: Press and hold the *Volume Up* and *Power* buttons simultaneously until the Samsung logo appears.
3. **Navigate to Wipe Data/Factory Reset**: Use the volume buttons to scroll down to *Wipe data/factory reset*. Press the *Power* button to confirm.
4. **Confirm the Reset**: Select *Yes* to confirm that you want to erase all data.
5. **Reboot Your Device**: Once the reset is complete, select *Reboot system now* to restart your device.

After performing a factory reset, your Galaxy S25 Ultra will be restored to its original settings, giving it a fresh start.

Keeping Your Device Updated with Software and Security Patches

Keeping your Galaxy S25 Ultra updated with the latest software and security patches is essential for ensuring optimal performance, stability, and protection against vulnerabilities. Here's how to manage updates effectively.

Automatic Updates

1. **Enable Auto Download**: Go to *Settings > Software update*.
2. **Enable Auto Download Over Wi-Fi**: Turn on *Auto download over Wi-Fi* to receive updates automatically whenever your device is connected to a Wi-Fi network. This ensures you're always up to date without manually checking for updates.

Manual Updates

1. **Check for Updates**: If you prefer to control when updates are installed, go to *Settings > Software update > Download and install*.

2. **Install Available Updates**: If an update is available, follow the on-screen instructions to download and install it. Your device will reboot if necessary to complete the process.

Update Notifications

1. **Stay Informed**: With *Auto download over Wi-Fi* enabled, you'll receive notifications whenever new updates are available.
2. **Manual Checks**: If you prefer to manually check for updates, remember to check regularly for any new software patches or updates that may have been released.

Update Benefits

- **Improved Performance**: Regular updates enhance device stability and speed, ensuring that your phone runs smoothly.
- **Security Enhancements**: Each update includes security patches to protect your device from potential threats and vulnerabilities.
- **New Features**: Updates often bring new functionalities and features, allowing you to enjoy the latest advancements.

By staying on top of software updates, you ensure that your device remains secure, efficient, and ready for any new features.

Accessing Samsung Support: Resources and Communities for Ongoing Help

When you need assistance with your Galaxy S25 Ultra, Samsung offers a range of support resources and communities to help you troubleshoot issues and maximize your device's potential. Here's how you can access them.

Samsung Support App

- **Download the Samsung Members App**: Visit the *Galaxy Store* to download the Samsung Members app. This app provides direct access to customer support, troubleshooting tools, and personalized advice based on your device usage. It also includes diagnostic tests to help identify and resolve common issues.

Online Help & FAQs

- **Visit Samsung's Support Website**: For quick answers to common questions, go to Samsung's official support website. You'll find troubleshooting guides, FAQs, and step-by-step solutions to resolve common problems.

Live Chat and Call Support

- **Connect with Samsung Support**: For more complex issues, visit the Samsung support page and enter your device details. You can initiate a live chat or call with a customer service representative for personalized assistance.

Samsung Community

- **Join the Samsung Community**: Visit the *Samsung Community* forum where you can discuss issues, share tips, and find solutions from other Galaxy S25 Ultra users. This is a great place to learn from the experiences of others and get real-time feedback on your questions.

Social Media and YouTube Channels

- **Stay Updated on Social Media**: Follow Samsung's official social media pages for the latest updates, product announcements, and tips. You can also visit Samsung's official YouTube channel for video tutorials, setup guides, and feature explanations.

Samsung Service Centers

- **Find a Service Center**: If your device requires repairs or professional service, use the Samsung Members app or the Samsung website to locate your nearest Samsung Service Center.

By using these resources, you'll have access to the tools and support you need to keep your Galaxy S25 Ultra running smoothly and solve any issues that may arise.

Chapter 11

The Future of Your Galaxy S25 Ultra

Future-Proofing: Maximizing the Lifespan of Your Device

Your Galaxy S25 Ultra is a significant investment, and taking steps to maximize its lifespan will ensure that it remains functional and efficient for years to come. Here's how you can protect and extend the life of your device.

Regular Software Updates

- **Stay Updated**: Samsung provides seven years of operating system and security updates for the Galaxy S25 Ultra. To ensure your device remains secure and performs optimally, install updates as soon as they're available.

Battery Care

- **Extend Battery Life**: The Galaxy S25 Ultra's battery is designed to last over 500 full charge cycles, retaining at least 80% of its original capacity. To keep it healthy, avoid letting your battery fully discharge, and refrain from keeping it plugged in for long periods after it's fully charged.

Physical Protection

- **Use a Case and Screen Protector**: While the Galaxy S25 Ultra features Corning Gorilla Armor 2 for durability, using a high-quality case and screen protector adds an extra layer of protection against accidental drops and scratches, preserving the physical integrity of your device.

Optimal Usage Practices

- **Avoid Extreme Conditions**: Keep your device away from extreme temperatures and high humidity, as these conditions can affect its performance and longevity.
- **Regularly Restart Your Device**: Restarting your phone occasionally helps refresh system processes, ensuring smoother performance.

- **Monitor App Performance**: Pay attention to apps that drain your battery excessively and remove or replace them if necessary to prevent long-term battery wear.

By following these simple practices, you can help ensure that your Galaxy S25 Ultra remains in excellent condition and continues to perform at its best for years to come.

Preparing for Future Android and Samsung One UI Updates

To ensure a smooth transition to future Android and Samsung One UI updates, it's important to prepare your device and data. Here's how to equip yourself for upcoming updates, keeping your device up-to-date and secure.

Understanding Update Policies

- **Samsung's Commitment**: Samsung promises seven years of operating system and security updates for the Galaxy S25 Ultra. This means you can expect major updates to Android and One UI through at least 2032, keeping your device equipped with the latest features and security patches.

Backup Strategies

- **Backup Your Data**: Before installing major updates, make sure to back up your important data to Samsung Cloud, Google Drive, or an external storage device. This step will protect you from potential data loss during the update process, ensuring that all your files, photos, and apps are safely stored.

Storage Management

- **Ensure Sufficient Storage**: Major updates can be large, so it's crucial to have enough available storage. Regularly clean up your device by deleting unused apps and files. For added space, consider transferring your media (photos, videos, documents) to cloud storage services like Google Drive or Samsung Cloud.

Staying Informed

- **Follow Samsung's Updates**: Stay updated on upcoming changes by regularly checking official Samsung channels, including the *Samsung Members* app, Samsung's website, and social media. You can also participate in beta programs to test new features early, but keep in mind that beta software may have some instability.

By following these simple steps, you'll be ready for future updates and can continue enjoying the latest features and security improvements on your Galaxy S25 Ultra.

Keeping Up with New Features and Technologies

To get the most out of your Galaxy S25 Ultra, it's important to stay current with new features and technological advancements. Here's how you can enhance your device experience by exploring new tools, apps, and accessories.

Exploring New Features

- **Review New Software Updates**: Regularly check for new features introduced in software updates. Samsung provides tutorials and guides to help you learn how to use these features effectively. Keeping up with the latest updates will ensure you're using your device to its full potential.

Third-Party Applications

- **Explore Complementary Apps**: There are countless apps that can enhance your device's capabilities. Consider exploring advanced photo editing tools, productivity enhancers, or fitness trackers that integrate seamlessly with your device. Always ensure that the apps are compatible with the latest software versions to ensure smooth performance.

Hardware Accessories

- **Enhance Your Device Ecosystem**: Accessories like the *Galaxy Buds* for high-quality audio or the *Galaxy Watch* for health tracking can significantly enhance your experience. Be sure to check compatibility with your current software before purchasing to ensure a seamless integration with your Galaxy S25 Ultra.

Community Engagement

- **Join Samsung's User Communities**: Stay informed and share experiences by joining Samsung's user forums and communities. You'll find valuable tips, real-time feedback from other users, and be the first to hear about the latest features and updates. This is a great way to learn new ways to make the most of your device.

By staying informed and exploring these new technologies and features, you can continually enhance your device experience, ensuring that your Galaxy S25 Ultra remains a powerful tool tailored to your needs.

Beyond the Galaxy S25 Ultra: Exploring the Samsung Ecosystem

Your Galaxy S25 Ultra is more than just a smartphone—it's the key to unlocking a powerful, connected digital ecosystem. Here's how you can expand your experience by integrating your device with other Samsung products.

Smart Home Integration

- **Control Your Home**: Explore Samsung's range of smart home devices, such as refrigerators, washing machines, and smart TVs. With your Galaxy S25 Ultra, you can control these devices remotely, making managing your home more convenient than ever. Imagine adjusting your thermostat or checking your fridge's contents directly from your phone.

Wearables and Health Devices

- **Sync with Samsung Wearables**: The Galaxy S25 Ultra pairs seamlessly with Samsung wearables like the *Galaxy Watch* and *Galaxy Buds*. Track your fitness, monitor your health, and receive notifications directly from your watch. You can also control music and access fitness data without needing to pick up your phone, providing a truly connected experience.

Samsung DeX and Ecosystem Integration

- **Transform Your Phone into a Desktop**: Samsung DeX allows you to turn your Galaxy S25 Ultra into a desktop PC, enhancing your productivity with a more desktop-like experience. When combined with devices like the *Galaxy Tab* or *Smart Monitor*, DeX becomes even more powerful, letting you manage tasks across multiple devices using a single interface.

Samsung Cloud and SmartThings Integration

- **Secure Your Data and Control Your Smart Home**: Use *Samsung Cloud* to back up your data and sync it across all your Samsung devices, ensuring your important files are always accessible. With *SmartThings*, you can also control various smart devices around your home, from lights to thermostats to locks, all through your Galaxy S25 Ultra.

SmartSwitch for Easy Device Transition

- **Quickly Transfer Your Data**: Switching to your Galaxy S25 Ultra is easy with Samsung's *SmartSwitch* app. Transfer contacts, photos, apps, and settings from your old device, making the upgrade process seamless and hassle-free.

By exploring the Samsung ecosystem, you can significantly enhance your digital experience, making your life more connected, productive, and streamlined. With all these devices working together, you'll be ready to take full advantage of the cutting-edge technology Samsung has to offer.

Conclusion

Wrapping Up: You're Now a Galaxy S25 Ultra Master!

Congratulations! You've completed your journey through this guide, and you're now equipped with the skills to fully maximize your Galaxy S25 Ultra. From setting up your device and personalizing your home screen to mastering advanced features like Samsung DeX and troubleshooting common issues, you now have everything you need to get the most out of your device.

With your newfound expertise, you can confidently navigate your Galaxy S25 Ultra, optimize its performance, and keep it running smoothly for years to come. Whether you're customizing settings, managing storage, or using the latest features, you're now ready to use your device like a pro.

But the journey doesn't stop here! Technology is always evolving, and there's always something new to discover. You've built a solid foundation, and now it's time to experiment with new features, stay updated with software improvements, and continue exploring all the possibilities your device offers. Your Galaxy S25 Ultra is a powerful tool—now that you know how to unlock its true potential, keep pushing the boundaries of what you can do with it.

So go ahead—take full advantage of your device, and continue to explore all the amazing things it can do!

The Next Steps: Continue Exploring, Experimenting, and Optimizing

Congratulations on mastering the basics of your Galaxy S25 Ultra! Now that you have a solid understanding of your device, it's time to continue exploring, experimenting, and optimizing to ensure you're getting the most out of your phone. The world of technology is always evolving, and so is your device.

Continual Exploration

With every new Android update, One UI feature, or app release, fresh opportunities to optimize and enhance your Galaxy S25 Ultra will arise. Stay curious and keep an eye on these updates as they roll out.

Exploring new features and functionalities not only keeps your device up-to-date but also helps you discover ways to improve its performance and tailor it to your needs.

Experimenting with Advanced Features

Now that you've mastered the basics, it's time to experiment with more advanced features. Take a deeper dive into tools like *Bixby Routines*, *Developer Options*, and automation features. Set up custom routines to automate tasks, explore hidden settings in Developer Options, or experiment with ways to enhance your device's functionality. Testing these features can open up a whole new world of possibilities that make your daily tasks smoother and more efficient.

Maximizing Efficiency

As you become more familiar with your device, you'll find ways to fine-tune it to fit your lifestyle. Optimize your workflow by adjusting settings like *battery-saving modes*, *notification management*, and *multitasking tools*. The more you experiment, the more you'll discover personalized ways to boost productivity and streamline your daily tasks. Don't be afraid to try new setups to see what works best for you!

The journey with your Galaxy S25 Ultra doesn't end here—it's just the beginning. By continuing to explore, experiment, and optimize, you'll stay ahead of the curve and ensure that your device remains a powerful tool for years to come. So go ahead, dive deeper, and push the boundaries of what your Galaxy S25 Ultra can do!

Additional Resources: Websites, Forums, and Communities for Ongoing Learning

To continue learning and enhancing your Galaxy S25 Ultra experience, there are many external resources that provide valuable insights, troubleshooting help, and opportunities to connect with other users. Here are some of the best places to expand your knowledge and stay up to date.

Samsung's Official Support Pages

- **Visit Samsung's Support Website**: For the most accurate and up-to-date information, head to Samsung's official support website. It offers FAQs, troubleshooting guides, and detailed customer support documentation.

Whether you're trying to solve a problem or explore new features, this is the most reliable resource.

Online Communities and Forums

- **Samsung Official Community**: Join Samsung's *official community* to discuss issues, share tips, and engage with other Galaxy S25 Ultra users. This forum is an excellent place for troubleshooting, discovering new features, and finding solutions to common problems.
  Reddit - Galaxy S25 Ultra Subreddit: If you prefer a more open, user-driven platform, the *r/GalaxyS25Ultra* subreddit on Reddit is a great place to interact with other Galaxy users. Discuss updates, new features, and ask for help with issues you encounter.

YouTube Tutorials and Reviews

- **YouTube for Guides and Reviews**: YouTube offers numerous video tutorials and device reviews that can help you better understand your Galaxy S25 Ultra. Channels like *Samsung Mobile* provide official guides, while independent tech enthusiasts give detailed walkthroughs on advanced features and troubleshooting.

Third-Party Resource Sites

- **Android Central**: This site is an excellent resource for Android enthusiasts, with detailed articles, reviews, and guides on the latest Android features and Samsung tips. It's a go-to source for in-depth explanations and optimization techniques.
- **XDA Developers**: Known for its expert-level guides and customization tips, XDA Developers offers extensive resources for those interested in diving deep into Android, from rooting devices to customizing software.
  XDA Developers
- **Lifewire**: Lifewire provides user-friendly tutorials and troubleshooting tips for Android devices, making it a great resource for both beginners and advanced users who want to optimize their devices.

By utilizing these resources, you can continue learning, getting the most out of your Galaxy S25 Ultra, and staying connected with the community for ongoing support. Whether you're troubleshooting an issue or exploring new features, these sites and communities will provide you with all the information you need to keep your device running at its best.

Appendix

Glossary of Key Terms

This glossary provides clear definitions of technical terms and concepts used throughout the guide. Understanding these terms will help improve your overall user experience and ensure you're making the most of your Galaxy S25 Ultra.

Battery Optimization
The process of managing power usage to extend the device's battery life. This includes using features like power-saving modes, reducing background processes, and limiting high-energy apps and services.

DeX (Desktop Experience)
A Samsung feature that allows you to connect your phone to an external monitor or TV and use it like a desktop computer. It supports mouse and keyboard input, making it ideal for productivity on a larger screen.

Bixby
Samsung's voice assistant that enables users to perform tasks, control apps, and get information using voice commands. Bixby can be activated with a simple voice prompt and can assist with tasks like setting reminders, sending texts, or controlling smart home devices.

App Drawer
An organized menu of all installed apps on the device. It is typically accessed by swiping up from the home screen, providing a quick way to access all your apps without cluttering the home screen.

5G
The fifth generation of mobile network technology, offering significantly faster speeds and more reliable connections compared to previous generations (4G and 3G). 5G supports high-bandwidth applications such as streaming, gaming, and faster downloads.

Wi-Fi Calling

A feature that allows you to make and receive calls using a Wi-Fi network instead of a cellular network. This can be especially useful in areas with poor cellular reception, as long as a stable Wi-Fi connection is available.

Secure Folder

A Samsung feature that allows users to store sensitive apps and files in a private, encrypted space on the device. It helps protect your personal data, such as financial apps and passwords, from unauthorized access.

These terms should help you navigate the technical aspects of your Galaxy S25 Ultra and make your device experience more intuitive and enjoyable.

Frequently Asked Questions (FAQ)

Here are answers to some common questions about your Galaxy S25 Ultra. These tips and solutions should help you resolve issues and optimize your device experience.

Q: How do I extend my Galaxy S25 Ultra's battery life?

A: To extend battery life, enable power-saving modes, reduce screen brightness, limit background apps, and disable unused features like Bluetooth and GPS when not in use. You can also enable adaptive battery settings, which will help limit power usage by apps you don't often use. For high-performance apps, consider reducing their use when possible.

Q: How can I improve the speed of my device?

A: Clear the cache and unnecessary data from apps by going to *Settings > Apps* and selecting the apps you want to clean. Disable or uninstall apps you don't use, and make use of the device's built-in performance optimization tools in the *Device Care* section. You can also restart your phone regularly to refresh system processes.

Q: What should I do if my device is overheating?

A: If your device is overheating, close any unused apps and reduce screen brightness. Avoid playing high-graphics games for long periods and ensure that your phone isn't exposed to direct sunlight or high temperatures. If the issue persists, give your phone a break to cool down.

Q: How can I back up my data?

A: To back up your data, use *Samsung Cloud* or *Google Drive* for automatic backup of your photos, videos, and documents. You can also manually back up files to these cloud services or use an external storage device. Always back up important data before performing any major updates or resets.

Q: How do I reset my Galaxy S25 Ultra?

A: To perform a factory reset, go to *Settings > General management > Reset > Factory data reset*. This will restore your device to its original settings, but remember to back up all important data before doing this, as it will erase everything on your device.

Q: Can I connect my Galaxy S25 Ultra to a TV?

A: Yes, you can connect your Galaxy S25 Ultra to a compatible TV. You can use *Samsung DeX* to transform your phone into a desktop experience, wirelessly mirror the screen via *Smart View*, or use a USB-C to HDMI cable to connect directly to the TV. Choose the connection method that works best for your setup.

By following these simple steps, you can keep your Galaxy S25 Ultra running smoothly and efficiently, addressing common issues and optimizing its performance.

www.ingramcontent.com/pod-product-compliance
Lightning Source LLC
La Vergne TN
LVHW060147070326
832902LV00018B/2996